RAMSHACKLE HOUSES

&

SOUTHERN PARABLES

BY KATHY BOLES-TURNER

Author's Note

Ramshackle Houses & Southern Parables was my first completed work as a writer. It was a rather consuming labor of love and regret that spanned twelve years from initial conception to final draft. After making the book available for print in September 2022, I immediately had another regret—not including my favorite poems and essays composed between 2017-2021.

Welcome to the 2nd edition.

Many thanks to the online publications who accepted individual poems to share with their audience, and all the writing friends who read and critiqued with patience and kindness. A special thanks to Quill, a prolific reader, writer, and painter who has never been embarrassed to admit she understands my labors of love and regret.

Thank you for reading.

Cover Design by nk_designing.
Cover photographs by Kathy Boles-Turner

VOLUME ONE

For Mama.
For tired mothers, factory workers, soldiers, and the open road.
All my favorite storytellers.

Volume One
Table Of Contents

MEMOIR

I journey

a journey that spans a sunlit churchyard

then stalls within a copse of oak

where daffodils lie trampled—I imagine—

by ambling ghosts

ambling over

from funeral dinners

laid out by old ladies who recall better days:

hazy Sundays sprinkled with hymnals

and yellow daffodil dresses.

ON GRANDPA'S LAND II

There was a rooster called Henry,
a hen called Red Hen,
and an old black dog
suspicious of them both.

Land and water sloped in a single direction;
sunflowers smiled toward the sky—loyal
'til the end. Summer rain sang
important songs ...

... as did the whippoorwill
counting souls
in narrow shadows.

On bare soles to the crick
(a journey past time and place).

"Be home 'afore the first whip-poor-will."

HEY DIDDLE DIDDLE

In my memories of the little white house on East Elm Street, it is always springtime. The people in my life are tall and prone to speaking in nursery rhyme when they notice that I am in ear shot.

Hey diddle diddle. /The Cat and the fiddle.

A sweet breeze sifts through window screens, billowing white sheers against warm yellow walls. Raggedy Ann, Andy, and a rescued stuffed monkey grin up at me from the floor.

I am four years old, and giddy with the prospect of my first day at Head Start. Atop my bed, freshly folded t-shirts, jeans, and new dresses are stacked in neat rows—Mama took me shopping.

The wonderful scents and bright colors of unsharpened pencils and tablet paper imprint upon my senses as I pack these new treasures into a red pencil box, then a denim book bag. I can read already, thanks to afternoons with Sesame Street and bedtime stories with Mama. I have learned a lot of stories.

The Cow jumped over the Moon.

To celebrate my first week in Kindergarten, Grandma McFerson sewed a blue dress with tiny yellow flowers on the shoulder straps. I feel very grown up. Especially when Mama presents me with a shiny prized possession to add to my second-hand books: a royal blue, over-sized copy of Mother Goose.

The little Dog laughed to see such sport...

Sweet breezes billowed white sheers against the yellow walls of my bedroom—the room where all my favorite stuffed toys and books lived; the room where I woke alone in the dark sometimes, hearing Mama and Daddy's voices shouting ugly words in the hallway.

Alcoholic. No rent money. It's all your fault. *And the Dish ran away with the Spoon.*

I know now that Kindergarten began in the fall. With the fall. Still, I remember it as springtime. The trees were full of songbirds, and puffy dandelion heads bobbed in cheerful clusters along the driveway.

Perhaps the lemon floor cleaner Mama used has colored my memories. Perhaps the walls weren't a soft yellow, or the little house so warm and lovely. Perhaps, when I looked up at the nighttime sky, I never saw a gleeful cow jumping a perfectly round moon.

We lived with Grandma for a while after leaving the little white house. When Daddy promised to be good, we all moved together to a place where the leaves remained brown and brittle long after Second Grade began.

Mama said that Mother Goose got lost in the move.

Hey diddle diddle. / The Cat and the fiddle.

DAYTIME DRAMA

Spectacles dangle at the tip of the bluebird's beak
as her feathered gloves point vigorous blame.
The squirrel fusses with the sleeves of her morning coat,
while sneering over such outlandish conjecture.

Laugher hides behind the fox's mustache.

Wren sisters have guessed the instigator's identity,
so they leave their weaving to whisper to the hawk,
who then conspires (much too loudly)
with the blood-lusting hound.

Vigilante justice is thwarted when the cat emerges,
in formal wear, to soothe the fray. "Peace can be achieved."

A visiting field mouse begs humbly to disagree,
hoping for alliance with the squirrel who lights a Winston and
declares the end of her patience.

"This neighborhood isn't what it used to be!"

The cat helps her pack for a more upscale residence ...
just above the fox's favorite hedge.

SUPER FRIENDS

Cherished with a third-grader's heart,
this routine, this quiet hour, means the world.
Costumed heroes wait in the living room
behind the screen of a second-hand TV.

She tiptoes past her mother's bedroom,
past a cranky gray cat curled low on the kitchen floor,
and with practiced stealth, climbs up high
to reach her favorite cereal bowl.

She concentrates on not leaving a trail of milk
to the perfect spot for viewing this weekend's
adventures of Wonder Woman, the Green Lantern,
the Justice League in all its glory.

Years will pass before she knows for certain
that Batman's outfit is black & gray, rather than lavender,
and Superman's cape is not such a dangerous orange.
Right now, none of that matters.

These champions are bright defenders
of innocence. They are the bravest, the most faithful
of friends. And they can be trusted to arrive
in the nick of time: Each misty Saturday morning.

Sunday afternoons in Grandpa's backyard,
boy cousins pretend to make single bounds.
They flick away villainous bullets, pose
in profile, skinny shoulders draped in stolen aprons.

They save the day and say things like,
"Aw shucks, it was nothing."
But every time she protests, "No, no, no!
you're doing it all wrong!"

And every time they sneer, "What do you know?
Go play with the other girls." To this she sighs
and shakes her head. "Poor dumb mortals.
Will you ever learn?"

Alas they never do. They never learn
to see past pigtails and a pale yellow dress—
her cape is fiery red.

THE TRUTH TELLER

I knew that Grandpa hadn't been the one to make my cousins believe that boys were better than girls. He was much smarter than that. So, I asked him who might have told the boys such awful lies. He frowned at me. The frown was a good sign—it meant he was taking his time to form the perfect answer.

He took his time in silence and gestured for me to sit beside him on the hill overlooking his garden. Finally, he said:

"The oldest of my people believed that men chose physical strength so they could hunt and defend their families. Women have a different kind of strength, and with it, they are given the secrets of Nature. Women long ago chose to be teachers of men, because it is they who know Nature and all of the peoples' purpose in it."

"Then girls *are* better than boys!"

"You will listen, or I will stop the telling."

"Yes, sir."

"Women have a different strength than men, a different eye, a different ear. They have great responsibility, as do men. We are meant to depend upon one another, to live in harmony and to enhance individual strengths. Men who listen well to their teachers become the greatest of leaders, because they grow to have the skills of warriors and hunters, as well as the hearts of Nature. And every nation that exalts the wisdom of women will flourish."

"Along the way of time, it happened that the children of great leaders forgot how their fathers became so strong; they forgot the value of the mothers and sisters, and so, the children don't listen well when they are corrected. The man and the woman are now at odds. This is bad."

"You're saying we're not supposed to argue over who is better than the other?"

"Exactly."

"And I'm supposed to help boys become great men."

"Exactly."

"Well, that's never going to happen."

"Don't be an ungrateful child among many, Granddaughter."

"Yes, sir."

I was eight years old then. The words he spoke that day played through my dreams over and over for several years. There were moments I would know the beauty and wonder of it all; there were days frustration got the better of me.

The night Death caught Grandpa off guard, he came to say goodbye to me. I sat up in my bed as he spoke the wisdoms stored up for years to come, and I listened as his voice grew sad and slow.

"I gave you alone the stories of the old people, yet you haven't saved them. You have not tried to share any of the truths, and there is no time left for me. As the stories remain unspoken, the forgetfulness lengthens, strengthens, and people will make their own histories to suit mistaken ideals. This is bad."

I absorbed this information as best I could, realizing that I would never hear my father speak with the same lyrical wisdom of his father. Tears choked back my words for too long.

"Wait! I'm just a kid. No one listens to me."

"Get their attention, Granddaughter."

"I ... I don't understand."

He left me there to grieve.

One night, soon after my fifteenth birthday, I heard his words echoing through memory—every story, every song. I hummed his songs and felt compelled to pick up pen and paper. When the first drop of ink touched the page, I finally understood.

TRAGEDY

Crisp, serene morning
Bore no semblance of warning
For what was coming.

HISTORY LESSONS

His mother long perceived life as a road,
his father, too, truth be known. The metaphor
was never questioned during their loving
parental lectures:

There is the road less traveled,
thin and thorny paths, and easy street.
The fast lane, the fast track; winding roads,
high and low. "Choose well," they said.

No mention was made of seeking safety
in ditches, or trenches. How a living body
might fit there while human horrors
stalk the wide-open roads.

When his boots are ordered to stop marching
through muck, through gore and ash, he unpacks
the nagging mystery of elder wisdom along with
dry socks and ammunition.

The gospel of trenches was delivered
just east of a tiny village a world away
from his mother's kitchen—a quick tutorial,
a short-handled shovel, and live grenades.

This is how a kid stays alive while flames bloom
above. He looks away from uphill battles
and sees himself wearing a graduation gown.
"Make us proud," they had said.

Decades later he shared war stories
riddled with plain common sense
for the sake of his wide-eyed grandkids:

"Don't be afraid to go out into the world
ready to dig some ditches. Make yourselves
proud," he said.

THE GOOD OLD DAYS

"Grandma, how old are you?"

"Well, I was born in aught-nine."

"What's *aught* mean?"

"It means oh. Nineteen-oh-nine. I was seventy my last birthday."

"Wow. You're older than Daddy's daddy, and I thought he was really old. Was 1909 back in the horse and buggy days?"

"Rich folks had horse n' buggies. We had a buck board and two mules. Hand me them shellin' peas, girl. I'm gonna show you how to do this right and we'll have us a good supper."

"Why don't old people go to the grocery store for their vegetables like everybody else?"

"A person gets real nourishment from their own gardens. When I was your age, I'd never seen an automobile nor a grocery store. I was too busy workin' the fields and doin' my chores."

"You didn't go to school?"

"Not past the second grade. Workin' to keep food on the table was for every member of the family."

"That must have been awful."

"What makes ya say that girl?"

"Working when you're a kid! How'd you learn to spell, or do long division? How can a little kid work in *fields* anyway?"

"My people had cotton. Brought the year's money and paid the landlord. By the time I was nine years old I was carryin' water for the pickers. By the time I was ten, like you are now, I worked a full day pickin'."

"I learned math in them cotton fields, girl. My folks got paid by the pound. Now listen, you gotta mind your fingers with these shellin' peas. Don't squish so hard."

"All right, I'll be more careful. You didn't miss school, Grandma?"

"Couldn't act like it workin' alongside the grownups. If I was to look wool gatherin' I'da got walloped."

"They *hit* you?"

"Kids get walloped. Gives 'em good sense. I've tried tellin' that to *your* mama but she won't listen. Reckon she'll regret that one day. Don't shake your head at me, girl!"

"Mama got real mad when you chased me with that switch. I've never seen her that mad. Did you wallop her for disobeying you? Even though she's a grownup?"

"Humph! Don't get your face all puckered now, 'course I didn't. She's got her own now. Her own responsibilities. I'll mind my business, even if I disagree. 'Ceptin' when you're on my property, you'll behave, or I'll get a switch after all. Guaranteed.

"There now, little girl! Them peas are done. We'll have a good supper tonight. Take this tub to the sink and bring me them snap beans."

"Yes ma'am. So, cotton is in the summer, right?"

"Pickin' ends in October sometimes, why?"

"Couldn't you have gone to school in the winter?"

"Some folks let their boys go to school durin' winter, some didn't. Fall and winter's hog killin' and late season vegetable tendin'. Takes a lotta work to put up pork, ya know. What are you shakin' your head about now, girl? Mind what you're doin' there, I want these beans in long strips, they go good with Irish taters."

"I don't think that's fair at all, Grandma—no school for girls. Besides, if you were working and gardening and killing animals all the time, when did you get to play?"

"Oh, we managed to have us some fun time to time. I was good at tag and just about any runnin' game, yes, I was. Once we was playin' tag between the cotton wagons and poor little Ellis—one of the neighbor boys—he was runnin' hell for leather 'cause I always won. He was runnin' so fast he didn't even see where his daddy had stacked up some hoes and the like. Well, Ellis tripped and fell right on a hoe blade and just nearly cut his left hand off. I declare! You sure can make some odd faces, girl."

"Grandma ..."

"Ain't you tired o' talkin' yet, child? I've had you in that garden all day long. A person would think you'd give out on words after all the questions you've asked. Why are you cryin'?"

"I sure am sorry, Grandma."

"About what? What's brought on such a neck huggin' as this?"

"I'm sorry you never got to be a kid."

YEAR THIRTEEN

Whiskey fume rivers
flooded in cold winter rains.
No lifeboats arrived.

GOSSIP

Great raging fires
would never spark if not for
a single whisper.

SAD CHILD

Insignificant bumps in the pavement

throw you down, beat you down.

Slight breezes blow you down,

bend and twist you around.

To devils you have no words to shout;

no thanks to angels slip from lips

sagging in a perpetual frown.

You'd better find a spine,

you'd best find a sign, a sound,

a golden crown to guide both feet

away from inevitable countdown.

SOME FORGOTTEN NAMES

1.
She clattered into the classroom
every time, with hair coiled like smoke,
brows drawn low—thunderclouds
of pure reproach. In her eyes we were not
merely eighth-grade impressionable minds,
but misery unleashed to damage her hard-earned
bliss. She devised fitting punishments.

2.
That much anticipated third first date
at seventeen escapes memory, maybe,
because his breath escaped too quickly—
in such a violent mournful way. Ragged
panting distracted from the goal of filing away
significant details. There were drinks and cloudy
ice cubes, loud music... then, hours later,
breakfast at a 'greasy spoon'. Egg yolk drowned
perfectly dry toast in the center of his plate, yet,
he seemed so happy.

3 & 4.
A pair of brothers who praised the historical
longevity and spiritual merits of weed: Each
wore blurry grins as they claimed CASH UP FRONT
was the usual standard of business, but since I am
a friend of a friend, they said, JUST THIS ONCE!
The transaction proceeded as paneling shook,
the windows shook, and they bragged in big
clumsy voices about their record collection.

NO ONE APPRECIATES VINYL THESE DAYS!
WE SHOULD DANCE, BLONDIE. YOU STILL
DATING WHATSHISNAME?

UNNOTICED

She never gave away her secrets.

It was at the river's edge
That she confessed,
Where she loosed the pain to drift
As gulls screamed and dove for prey.

You never noticed her go missing.

HOW TO ESCAPE A MONSTER

Remember:

When brain and skull collide
Sunshine-colored dots
Ooze down into red red;
Bottomless black will soon threaten.

Beware the black.
There you will be defenseless
Against terror unmatched by fists,
And teeth in sulfur-scented whispers.

Quiet as heartbreak, wait.
Don't waste screams for help.
Refuse the lure of anger
Or sorrow, hatred, or hope.

Never taunt with pleas for mercy—
Just wait. Gather strength.
Opportunity will arise
When the monster blinks.

Freedom will flash against
Fading red red, I promise. In that moment,
Put both feet fast to the cold hard ground,
Don't stop. Don't look back.

DON'T LOOK BACK

That woman missed her true calling. She belts out a series of screams that would shame Hollywood's most famous horror movie queens. She won't stop. Can't stop.

I possess astounding clarity in these few moments and wonder how long it will last.

The screaming woman's reception area leads into a rectangle office that smells of pipe smoke and dust. I want to borrow the phone.

Brassy light hurts my one good eye. I realize rather calmly that the other one is swelled shut and may be permanently ruined. Footsteps thunder behind me. I don't even flinch; I just continue dialing an almost forgotten number.

"Mama. Will you come get me?"

"Where are you… is someone screaming? What happened?"

"It's just the secretary. I'm at the factory off Highway 57."

The secretary's screams turn to shouts, "Oh my god! Did you see her face? Oh my god!"

"Mama?"

"I'll be there in an hour, baby. Do you need anything?"

"The Sheriff. And. Maybe a doctor."

A man's voice makes the atmosphere around my head begin to

buzz red again. My vision goes dark. I hate the dark. I might miss something important.

When my vision returns, that man is inches away. Harry? Howie? The foreman. He smells of cherry pipe tobacco and he looks really pissed off.

"We should call the police. I don't want to be responsible for you, girl."

"Fuck off, will ya? I'm fine." Did I say that? Apparently. His face is blustery as he turns away. I think I might throw up.

Another face blurs in my damaged peripheral. His voice is sweet as spring water.

"I want a description of who did this to you, sugar."

Time is lost. I'm lucid then I'm lost. The air sparks and melts away. I hear Mama's voice before I see her. Her whole body shakes as she hugs me.

***

"So, he beats the tar out of you last night then makes a twenty-minute drive before dawn to drop you off at work?" The Sheriff's smirk is wide and ugly. He turns toward a fat deputy and actually winks. "I guess that ole boy has finally gone qualified crackers. He usually tries to cover his messes better."

My mother's voice cracks the paint on the walls. "Do you mean to tell me he's beaten up other girls? Why isn't he in jail?"

"Same reason he won't go to jail this time. *They* never testify against him. And no, it's not always girls. He put that Harper boy in a coma three years ago. A lead pipe, wasn't it, Emmons?"

The fat deputy chuckles, "Yessir. Witnesses testified in that one. Little shit got a good lawyer, though. Didn't serve three weeks."

The Sheriff graces us with another smirk. I stare back at him with my good eye.

"Oh, he's a sweet talker, that one. Your girl will be back on his property in thirty days. I'd bet money. Go on to the doctor, now. Get some x-rays."

My throat feels raw and bloody. "I want an order of protection... or... whatever that's called."

His smirk dies. He leans forward and levels a hard set of eyes on me. "You won't be wasting any of my paperwork, girl. Come talk to me in thirty days. Not a minute sooner."

My tiny one-hundred-pound mother is forcibly escorted out of the Sheriff's office by three deputies. I follow behind on wobbly legs.

***

I've had enough with people's horrified stares and barely concealed contempt. I refuse to go to the E.R.

Mama still has that tone in her voice that makes me hate myself. "Why didn't you tell me you were being abused?"

I have no answer.

Time is distressingly fluid. I float in and out of consciousness, voices hum electric. My mind claws through syrupy blackness, struggling to piece together all the lies I've told. I am not safe.

"What day is it?"

Someone answers from miles away, "You've only been here for eight hours."

"I need to leave. Now."

My little brother is suddenly there, swiping tears off his cheeks as he hands me a glass of water. "Your throat must hurt real bad, huh?"

Mama demands, "What do you mean you need to leave?"

This fear will be the death of me. "He knows by now. That I've gotten away. He'll come here first."

Her eyes flash like sun against glass. I know that she is plotting his murder, sure as if she'd confessed aloud.

"Don't Mama. Just take me somewhere, please. I'm a danger to all of you. I would go alone... but I don't think..." The air turns liquid. I float away.

My sister swims by, "I know where to take you."

***

The movement beneath me is not a sinking boat. I look out a window and recognize the driveway. "Here?"

My sister speaks miracles, "He never met them, so he can't know to look here. I called Mrs. King, she's expecting us. Don't worry."

Mrs. King is the mother of my best friend from kindergarten. I haven't seen either of them for years. She is the first person to not look at me and cringe or condemn. She smiles and opens her arms.

"Hello, sweetheart. Let's get you a warm bath."

***

I have to ask the name of each day. I have difficulty piecing together what they mean. People talk to me, plead with me, but I slip away to a place where quiet thunders in my ears and big thumbs press against my larynx. I can't breathe.

Then the tart smell of lemons brings me alive while a soft cool cream massages the gashes and bruises on my face. Mrs. King is singing. I relax.

"Sweetheart, you need to get up. He found you."

Not a hint of panic constricts her voice. She has a pistol in her left hand.

"Get up. We're going to take you somewhere safe."

***

The sun scorches my raw skin. I look across an immaculate lawn to where a distinguished old courthouse sprawls. There is cold hard ground beneath my feet.

Today is the day I testify.

IF ONLY

If only I could cry you an ocean
so you might sail away, or sink
and set me free of all your sins,
and yours, and yours.

If only dry sobs didn't roughen
my throat, and scar my words
of introduction into new circles
that don't thrive on hate

and fear, and hunger.
If only I could have been born
to another era, just down the road
from here, in a time when wisdom

flowed from mother's milk, not through
hot wires of hard learning. If only
someone had taught me how to pray
earlier, miracles might have saved us all.

ON GRANDPA'S LAND III

Leaves rustle up the scent
of damp Tennessee soil,
and from somewhere
deep in memory I hear his voice.

I see my eight-year-old face
through his eyes; the frayed
edges of his reflection passes mine,
and I know that I am safe.

"Grandpa, why do sunflowers
look as if they're grinning at the sun?"

"Because that is exactly what they're doing."

In those years of tender youth
I lived inspired by his faith in magical truths.
Now his wisdom doesn't fit between the lines
of real life without hard-earned proof.

SHILOH

When sunrays succumb to a pink blaze,
and the moon is only a dim sliver, cool
evening dew drops outline boot prints
marching that battleground.

When blue-gold light comes to linger
in the trees, at ease soldiers gather round
the ghost of a campfire, no longer weary,
no longer thirsty. They are not afraid.

Voices mingle in laughter and song; voices
rise and fall like smoke, like memories.
As tree lights begin to faint away, men young
a hundred years and more speak of home.

They share the leathery touch of a mama's bible,
the wide steady shoulders of a laboring father,
and the advice of a stranger traveling from long ago:

Bless your children with strong names, and bless
yourself by keeping faith in those vows made
to God, not governments.

Uniforms and glory don't matter here. Gold stars,
tattered flags and skin color do not hold rank
anymore, as the lives bled into that battleground
gather around the ghost of a campfire.

MIRROR MIRROR

Behind the color that swims in your eyes,
beneath false laughter that lingers in the air
is a hint, just a whisper of lies.

The way your mouth curves at the corner
tells me that you nod and smile
in the guise of another—

there remains a secret that you cherish,
that you guard with charm and words
long loveless and barren.

Is it a cumbersome thing?

Does it weigh you down with worry;
echo in your mind as you sigh
with false sincerity?

I see what you are doing.

Spin a tale and sparkle
in flattering light. Fool the fools
as they marvel.

This mask, it must be stifling.

Turn to me fully so that I may see—
reality shines best in gray morning light.
You can trust me.

YESTERDAYS

We drive with the windows down
Letting sticky August fingers tangle our hair.
Ribbons of dust and gravel wave alongside
Miles of spent cotton rows.

Ramshackle houses, eyeless and idle,
Stand guard over engine block boneyards.
Rusted fenders and cinder blocks shade old dogs
Sniffing out a familiar stench.

We drive past bent neighbors, vacant,
Staring at nothing but their troubles.
Along the way he tries to sing my favorite song
But I'd rather hear the radio.

On past the riverbed and unmarked graves,
We drive with the windows down, watching
As dark curtains pull across the flat blue sky
And all the constellations ignite.

When we drive past the county line
His sex and velvet voice says you know I love you.
And in my own distant way I say, love me,
If you want to. Just keep driving.

THE BREAKFAST SHIFT

Sun sweats against east windows,
pressing shadows atop 2-tops and 4-tops
bolted to a swath of ugly green carpet.

She suspects her uniform
is woven from the same materials
as that repulsive, neglected carpet:
Polyester/ Ranch Dressing/ Mystery Dye #5.

But there is no time to investigate. Her pace
is set to the unceasing rhythm of scraping forks
and voices threatening to cut.

Parallel parades of burnt orange booths
march front-to-back-to-back, each
packed with revenant ravenous folk
who know her by name.

"Hey, Babe!" They shout out loud
while sopping at their plates,
while stabbing blame at empty coffee cups.

The hookers, weary at dawn;
bankers and buyers on the look out
for the weak. The sellers and tourists,
armed with pretense—

All gather upon burnt orange vinyl
buffed to a grimy sheen of swapped DNA.
She worries that every fiber of her soul
might be stained just the same.

Late afternoon light undulates across
south windows. Fresh air wafts in, to splinter
walls of coffee musk, to splinter her pace.
At last, she is free to leave.

She takes home soiled cash and a bloody taste
on both hands, wondering, how will it all come clean?

READ ME

Pretend I am coveted combustible data;

I am the very words you must have.

As if I were written on the purest imported paper,

place me gently among your favored volumes.

Let your lips move in heated whispers as you read me.

WEDDING DAY

Gardenia petals litter a narrow walkway meant for the bride. This is her mother's house—a pretty little cottage surrounded by blazing azaleas and big, gnarled oaks. Rain clouds bear down from angry April skies, dimming the vibrant colors of the wedding décor inside.

Children wearing their Easter best run barefoot through carpeted rooms. Long before the ceremony, four-year-old flower girls have scattered the contents of their baskets and smeared their skirts with cake icing, giving away their secret.

Upstairs, the bride isn't blushing. The mother of the bride is tearfully recounting a list of her daughter's many bad decisions, pacing the floor, nervous and pleading. The older woman appears frail in her delicate white dress and delicate white shoes, but the daughter knows better.

"There's still time to call this off. Don't be stubborn."

The bride turns away to fill a glass and demands, "Enough, Mama. For *Christ's sake!* It's just a little rain."

"Rain is bad luck on a wedding day."

"Since when do you quote Grandma's superstitions?"

"Me? For two weeks you've been repeating, 'get married in blue and your love will always be true', over and over as if to convince yourself this one will work out. Look at what you're wearing! Who puts the wedding party all in white while the bride wears navy blue? And no flowers? No catering? Your photographers are twelve-year olds! Twice already I've heard guests whispering about what mess this is."

"Enough! Mama. I swear you'll make me a raving lunatic if you don't quit. Go get those brats away from the cake, or something."

"I guess it won't matter what happens. If you don't put that whiskey down, you're liable not to remember anything at all about your own wedding anyway."

With a burning, judgmental glare, the bride's mother leaves her alone.

The wedding wasn't intended to be grand. She'd wanted home and hearth and a casual celebration. Patriotic ribbons and sentimental music. She'd wanted...

"What the hell am I doing? What have I let him talk me in to? I never wanted this any of this. "

True. For an entire year she evaded his proposals. She protested his conventional ideals, argued that love and marriage cannot coexist, that love doesn't always age well. He would not be swayed.

She only gave in because it became obvious that he meant every promise. It became obvious that he is not a hopeless romantic. For him, this is the only feasible next step—you marry the one you love. She gave in because she feared if they didn't marry, she would lose him.

"I can't go through with this!"

Heart beating as if it might shatter in her chest, she runs toward the room where he is getting dressed, determined to put a stop to all this nonsense.

A clap of thunder announces her entrance, and there he stands in crisp dress blues. His face shines with the best smile ever invented as he says "Hey, sweetness. Are you ready?"

Something in her soul quiets the instant she hears his voice. Suddenly, that is all the reason she needs.

She returns his smile and says, "Let's go get married."

HONEYMOON

Sapphire blue bay in early May—beauty that storms the eye. Try to drink your fill. Will you promise to savor these moments, save them from the fog of future memories, keep them for the sake of you and me?

Me and you bounding over grapevine hills, concrete loops, white powder sand, we laugh as if nothing would dare change our route. Doubt is for losers, not lovers. Cover me. See the battleships at peace, winking at one another across the bay?

Weigh your words; they mean everything now. How is it that these hours, these days might remain divine—like a road trip into God's own mind? Find those blurry photographs we took at full speed. Heed the signs driving past, west-to-east, down below turquoise skies pointing us back home.

DISLOCATED

Home on the range!

> Well, not exactly the *range*
> and not exactly *home,*
> but exactly where we landed.

Schizophrenic weather pummeled me toward suicidal tendencies during that first undefined season, yet an undeniable need to nest took me over inside an old house that harbored no one's ghosts. Outside, weeds hacked at my hands as I forced flowers into unforgiven soil. Nothing bloomed in that air bleached out and dried by raw sunlight. I couldn't find a way to mourn

> where it's too arid for crying,
> even when winter scratched
> against barren windows.

Frustration began to burn akin to spring, so I dug out beauty with a Kodak then sat back on collected yard sale finds with some measure of satisfaction, until dreams consisting of damp blanket air and nonthreatening sunrises woke me, providing unfair amounts of time to endure shards of rock glinting in

> brushfire winds,
> and the surround sound
> of rattlers fending off prey.

Defeated, near death it seemed, I traded tired and allergic garden tools for a pen, then a keyboard that clicked relentlessly at all that I had left unexamined. Facts

> about a foggy past,
> and how to put flowers
> into poetic form.

True comfort can't be found outside these walls, but only in the arms of a partner who doesn't give a wit for foggy pasts or flowers or poems. He's got a thing for my eyes and often strives to make me snort rather than laugh a simple laugh. It is he, after all, who has vowed to help me harvest a sense of home

> no matter where we go.

ECONOMICS

A wise investment:
Mercy. Store it up today
for tomorrow's sake.

THE SOUND OF WRITING

A metallic grinding.
    A slick wine-greased giggle.
      A thundering gallop
        over that last towering edge.

A silence so dense with awe
    the sun dares not move
      songbirds wait to sing
        and breezes hold their breath.

A keening mournful wail
    that steels a heartbeat
      robs hope and drives
        the best of men to suicide.

The flutter of silken wings. The searing sting of a hollow
point. The visceral smack of failing organs bleeding out.
Flatline.

Writing will wake you with whispers. Make crazed
accusations. Lecture threaten and plead. Listen.

ADVICE FROM A PROPHET

Take this moment—hold it close.
Let its heat flood your veins and seep
down your bones. Warmth bears color
and texture to be treasured.

Now, pull away.

Take this moment—hold it at arm's length,
examine every sharp edge. Measure its width
and breadth. Run your fingers across the face
as it cools and solidifies.

Now, turn it toward the light.

Pose this moment before a camera— capture its angles,
its sorrow, for benefit of future skeptics. Shadows
will challenge natural light, that's okay. Be true
to the process. Savor the process.

Now, frame your favorite image.

Study this moment—hang it center of a blank wall.
When you know every pixel, take up a pen to speak
the emotions that water your eyes. Love will shine
in the ink, as will the shadows.

Now your moment is immortal.

THE SUN'S FAVORITE SEASON

Ethereal love—
Autumn's daylight is *romance.*
That graceful pale gold
gives "beauty" definition:
A sweet falling tenderness.

PEOPLE

People have a way of smiling while choking
on self-loathing. People have a way of jumping
down rabbit holes when magic waits in plain sight.

People have a way of having it all but settle for dining
on cold fare then skipping dessert. People have a way
of disappearing in their own reflections.

People have a way of spilling sadness into 100-proof
bottles. People have a way of blinking just as the best
things in life pass by. People have a way of never knowing

why love is so hard to hold in a two-handed grip.

CHOICE

Humankind suffers
no real shame in the profit
of free will: it's choice
to save ourselves from ourselves.
Choice creates art from ashes.

[NO] SURRENDER

The poet advises wise men,
grave men, wild men, good men, to fend off
the dying of the light. What of the "fairer"?

What of those for whom wars are claimed
and sins are blamed? What of the mothers
and daughters these wise and wild, grave
and good men leave behind, once defeated
by the threat of darkening night?

What advice have you, poet?

Speak to me of dignity,
of frail deeds and purpose. Will you not speak
as if I know the meaning of bravery?

No.

And so you leave me with no wisdom
to glean from men. Nevertheless, I do not relent.
Goodbye, poet. Goodbye.

GLOW

Van Gogh got drunk on yellow and drew a map to the heat

of God's hollow eye. He crashed against eleven melting stars,

then slipped inside silken folds of a midnight cape designed

to hide one fierce dragon and a web of broad irons

that confine madness to terrible heights.

This is how Anne Sexton wants to die:

swallowed up by that rushing Beast

of Van Gogh's boiling night.

I want to stay alive to taste the yellow.

PANIC

Cigarette smoke swirls above her furrowed brow.

Left alone in the quiet,
she stares at nothing nearby,
while dust raises crooked fingers
in dark corners;

dirty dishes copulate
against stainless steel bedding,

and photo-shopped memories—
magnetized and smiling—
preoccupy the recesses of her mind.

Ceiling fans whir all hours
hypnotizing a radio
left alone to drool static.

Plans for happiness have been dulled,
in this old house. Now, her lone monotone
repeats Eliot's forlorn verses:

I have measured out my life with coffee spoons;
voices dying with a dying fall
Beneath the music from a farther room
So how should I presume?

Panic fades
as she becomes faithful to the pain.
After all, monogamous relationships
require certain dedication.

[UNTITLED]

With cool fingers she
unravels the silvered threads
of his last riddle.

Where does he find time
to work out the game—this game
of unwritten rules?

She needs words, structure,
bullet points, graphics—graphics
would be helpful, yes.

Silk threads—cruel proof
of failure tangle intent.
He smiles. She smiles back.

I WILL KNOW YOUR LOVE WAS REAL

Please refrain from metaphors
Made of heart-shaped paper,
And I will know your love was real.
Describe it glistening with viscera,
                    Not rose-scented.

Authentic emotion is far removed
From that bloody muscle laced with blue veins...
It's down beneath the pasty brown stink
Of the liver, in the vicinity of the appendix,
That love throbs and twists—where it thrives
Or dies.

That muscle to the north
Keeps pumping on, uninterrupted,
Unaffected, as love gets ripped from the gut.

A HOBO'S EPIPHANY

The search for hope led me westbound
to a worn, but lonesome road. Years passed on,
miles trudged by uncounted, until my soles longed
to be bare in the lavender dusk of one September evening.

I had come to a place where tall grasses rested
beneath the wounded arms of an ancient tree, and there
I fell down to dream of a brittled widow wearing
her wedding gown. Satin fabric frayed in a razor wind
as the widow dropped apples into a basket.

I dreamed with a smile, wishing for her to sing,
but, alas, the moon's glower woke me before that first note.
In the fierce white light bearing down, I witnessed
tall grasses bow and saw stars turn their backs.

It was then I heard feathered prophecy approaching—
He is a bearer of secrets, the Owl, and the one I have sought.
It seemed the old tree knew this divine messenger well,
for she lent a shoulder to serve as His perch.

That razor wind returned from my dream;
the tree hummed softly. The cold dark backs of stars
dangled in the sky, and the moon's stare stiffened.
In that moment I knew the Owl had come for me.

Breathless, I chanced at look at his face; He looked back at me with yellow mystic eyes. I bent my head to make a vow: "Please speak and I will listen." At last, He whispered with God's own voice. He said, *"Go on home now,"* and I shivered.

EVOLUTION

In the shade of your masculine stare, my *self* begins to flourish.
People who notice say I am a radiant bride:
so pretty, so young, so full of passion.

I am eager for the future.

In the electric gloom of your fortieth year, my *self* is pallid.
People who notice claim I am a good wife:
willing, dependable, transparent.

Our future is tangled in the past.

In the fragile dawn of your return, my *self* is mine.
People don't know what to say.

THE BEST LAID PLANS

I.

I learned to live alone in an old yellow house by burning
baggage that wouldn't go cheap at a last chance yard sale.
Some troubles won't leave easy; some troubles can't find
the right kind of lowest bidder, so, I set fire to what was left.

II.

Neighbors came out to see how high the flames might leap.
They expected explosions, I imagine.

I stood between my first bonfire and the yellow house I
loved so much; I stood in the shadows, watching as pencil
sketches unfurled in trails of blue smoke.

No one else noticed my childhood drawings drift up in the
ghost white moonlight. Memory unbidden began to fill in
careful outlines—bittersweet tries, night after night, of
drawing out the many bricks that built my dream houses.

III.

Daddy always settled for cold water rentals with dirt yards
and crooked porches. He was free from ambition and clever
notions, had no need for creature comforts like warm baths
poured straight from the tap.

What mattered was a steady flow of drink between paychecks. Leaky roofs and drafty windows paid the price, bottle-to-bottle. We went like nomads from one ramshackle house to another, so I toiled away, building sturdy ranch-style houses on scratch paper—real homes we didn't have to leave when the rent came due.

Each penciled version had neat rows of flowers, and a pretty veranda facing steamy sunrises. My dream houses had leak-proof roofs, not a single drafty window, and a river wandering by.

Daddy would find me at my work and say stop wasting paper.

IV.

Do you remember our Midtown apartment? And that awful trailer out in North Carolina? I feared for us at first. I feared our marriage would end up like theirs—just an ugly series of sad, temporary shelters.

My fears were unfounded. You are a good man with no real love for the bottle, and I have always been fond of flowers and haggling for vintage furniture. We traveled from coast-to-coast, you and I, and I kept on designing dream houses.

Those later drawings were in ink—solid plans for old age, complete with rocking chairs on the veranda. You never demanded I stop dreaming. You never asked me to suffer life without in cold water rentals. I made that last trip out west harboring a mournful heart, knowing that rivers can't wander through those flattened landscapes.

Maybe it was kismet that brought us to the yellow house—
an old farm had been razed, years before, but the house
saved. It stood on a well-treed corner lot under a faded
denim sky, and I knew then our rocking chairs should be red.

V.

I packed away my baggage, at last, and went to work pruning
trees. Fat mums took root, somehow, in that rough soil. You
seemed proud. It took one full year to cultivate a lawn, just
as long to furnish those big old rooms. I hung photographs
on the walls and bought treasures all over town. Four more
years went by, and it all would have been perfect if I could
have made you stay.

VI.

Maybe it was my fault. I'm still not sure.

Maybe I should have kept planning to build, instead of
accepting the good fortune of finding a dream house sitting
on a corner lot, waiting. Did I get lazy? Or, what's that word
you kept pointing ... complacent?

VII.

I learned to live alone.

The pain almost made me deaf. Summer wilted everything,
quietly, but the autumn flowers came in nicely, and just one
Elm died in December's fierce ice.

I spent weeks writing dark poetry—much like that of a distant adolescence—and I prayed a lot. By year's end I had a new sketchbook and sometimes felt guilty for being all right in the silence.

VIII.

I got another dream house all drawn out. There were flower beds, a library, a guest room, and a garage, because you know I hate scraping winter off car windows.

A river wound its way slow and sluggish, south and east. I made the plans, step-by-step, to go back home, back to green hills and steamy early mornings.

With the news that I was moving, neighbors came out in crowds to buy some of the treasures and troubles I sold. I set fire to the rest and stood in the shadows watching the smoke.

IX.

You called as I crossed the state line. I listened to the road as you demanded I turn around; I apologized and hoped you'd hear my sorrow. I kept driving.

X.

Months later, we got together for a drive down past the ruins of my childhood, and I told you stories that didn't rhyme. You listened to every one as we shared a bottle, then two, and another.

Reconciliation came at a cost—we changed.

In the end, it was worth all the pain. It was worth burning up baggage and driving east. I no longer draw my dream houses because you followed me home.

UNCHARTED

With gentle hands

and a strong voice, steady

eyes and a resilient heart,

go the way you must.

VOLUME TWO

For Uncle Dickey and those rare, freely given life lessons.

Volume Two
Table Of Contents

JOE COOL

My grandmother's acre-wide lawn, lush green beneath a baby blanket sky, was kept neat and trimmed by her youngest son—my uncle, my favorite. Even at six years old I noticed his difference. I was frequently disappointed by adults, their tiresome demands for obedience and respect. He demanded nothing. Simultaneously youthful and all-knowing, amidst the noise and busy preoccupation of other adults, he wore a quiet smirk and never gave in to the temptation to lecture me.

Maybe it was his lack of demands, or his handsome cuffed shirts; maybe, the ever-present dark lenses and chrome frames disguising his inherited sharp blue eyes. Maybe it was the way every surface willingly accommodated his penchant for nonchalant leaning. Whatever the primary indicator, it was obvious even to one so young as I that he was *cool*.

He took the time to train his awkward little basset hound to count. Mutt (the hound was lovingly called) would bark twice when two fingers were held up, four times for four, and so on. Mutt could climb a ladder, drive the riding lawn mower, and would happily pose for photos wearing shades and a cap. No other grown up I've known, then or since, possessed the patience or the insight to tend to a homely old awkward dog until its genius is revealed for all to witness.

I was the type of kid that tried the nerves of taller folk—teen babysitters to elderly grandparents, and all in between. So they often told me. Visiting relatives were warned upon arrival: don't mind Kathy, she'll ask you why and how until your hair falls out. During these dire declarations, as the visitors backed away warily, my favorite uncle would place a hand atop my head and remain reassuringly silent. Later on, when the visitors were sure to see, he would create an opportunity for me prove worthy of their admiring attentions.

I would accompany him to the garden to bring in vegetables, climb the peach tree for dessert ingredients, command Mutt to do all his tricks for the audience, read aloud a joke from the Reader's Digest, or listings in the TV Guide. He would smirk and level dark glasses on these visitors until they admitted with beaming smiles that I was well behaved and possibly the smartest kid they'd ever met.

Best of all—unique in my world dominated by exasperated adults—when he wanted to be free of my company, he would take off his shades, look me in the eye and say, go away now. A kid can't help but admire a straightforward grown up.

It may have been my baby brother who first called our uncle Joe Cool, I can't remember with certainty. Regardless, no other nickname in the history of nicknames was ever so suitable. Years went by. Five became eight, then ten, then twelve. His coolness never wavered; my admiration sometimes turned to envy.

I craved his easy quietness, his penchant for nonchalant leaning. My regret mounted as I couldn't, no matter how I practiced before the mirror, achieve that all-knowing smirk. And I never could convince any of my puppies to do more than sit or chase a stick.

When he drove over for visits, sacrificed his time to "just because" shopping sprees with me and my sister, or drove us all around for Mama's errands, or took us on day trips to a state park, I would observe him closely. The realization of momentary shyness, obligation to protect, or tension around my father only compounded my appreciation.

He passed on a lot to me, including how to mow a lawn, a love for great stereos and vintage cars. My appreciation didn't waver when it became obvious, he didn't possess the steely nerves required for teaching me to drive. I have to admit my own fault for that since it seemed impossible to listen to his soft-spoken wisdom once my foot was near an accelerator. I did manage to absorb his lessons on car care, and lawn care, though, which is knowledge that's served me well throughout my own adulthood.

Why can't more adults be like him? Why can't I? The years have continued to tumble away. He is now well past the age as my first memories of Grandma, getting frail, coughing when he laughs. We haven't been on a road trip or shopping spree in ages. And I've yet to teach a dog to count.

GENERATION GAP

Mama's mama was told girls don't have time for school. They cook, clean, pick cotton, marry and give birth. Daddy's daddy

was told to check white in the race box when he enlisted. The Cherokee don't matter anyway. Both barely survived that

glorious era, that wondrous age of WW2. Mattie, given years before to a stranger, a sharecropper, bore her 7th child in '45.

JD sweated out nightmares and cheap beer on the voyage west, leaving Europe in ruin. He had a uniform, medals and

papers to prove he'd served old Uncle Sam. Surely, he could get a job somewhere. Mattie's 10th came into the world while

Korea still smoldered. By then, JD was drinking his dinners in North Memphis bars before walking home to the wife and

kids. About the time Vietnam set afire, Mattie's elderly husband fell ill. They would never own that poor patch of land

farmed for forty years. She was tired anyway, tired of her daughters asking why the colored folks got paid for field

work, but not them. She got cheap rent in North Memphis, and doctors close by, not to mention a growing list of sons-in-law

that didn't have to depend on hateful old cotton. Soon after Mattie and JD became neighbors, he was publicly declared a

white man—in a chorus of riot voices as shots rang out. The streets were turning to war more and more. He had to get

away. Black and white, let the devil take 'em all, he said, then headed east to McNairy where the land sloped and sold cheap.

Just a while after I came along, Mattie and JD became neighbors again—ten country miles apart. By then, her belly was

perpetually swollen, her legs bent. She told stories about a childhood that made me cry and she had little patience for questions. I had thousands of questions. JD's stooped shoulders did not straighten when he faced his grown children, nor when

he walked his own land. That time killing Germans afforded him a small pension, and a year-round garden never quite

fenced off from the chickens. He sang in a different language when he thought no one was listening. I was always listening.

They were my first loves, first storytellers, favorite historical figures. Both cared enough to notice that I would do anything,

swear anything for them: Mattie made me promise to get good grades and never trust a man. JD dared me to stay fearless.

YOU ARE. HE IS. SHE WAS.

You are aftermath: the sizzle and hum riding low
over scorched fallow fields, center of nowhere.

He is golden streetlights keeping count
(desperate to keep count) for miles and miles.

She was the crack and flare of a burned-out bulb
that left you stunned, hand still on the switch.

You are marmalade on my fingertips
about to be licked away. Don't go.
He is yesterday's migraine.
He is the migraine medicine.
She was the lost rule book—
dogeared pages & smeared ink.

You are silver-edged, misty mornings with
good coffee and cozy socks.
He is a laughing baby, the scent of newspaper.
She was shelter against the weather—
a tin roof rain danced down.

You are hello.
He is so long, see you around.
She was always ready for a road trip.

YOU CAN'T HAVE MY LAST
CIGARETTE

Radio songs play true love out
to a beat, childish and hollow.
With a smirk, I'll paraphrase:
I'd live and die for you, morph
into a superhero, become the sun

and moon, just for you. Truth is
we'll both live and die while the sun
is still the sun and the moon is still
the moon. Love won't stop me from
telling the truth, so pack away those

tights, babe, and keep on looking fly
in business casual. Keep on bringing
home those benefits like a real hero.
Romance ain't dead, it just looks a lot
different than the radio believers

pretend. It plays out a bit offbeat, like
this: I will take care of your dogs, always.
I will walk to the ballpark on date night
with sore knees. I will drive in the rain
to gas up the cars when you've got the flu.

I won't hazard a guess at how long we'll
be together beneath that fading sun and
gloomy moon. Truth is, you can be quite
the dick and I can't seem to stop this mud
slide from hot rocker chick to fragile old

lady. In moments of doubt, memories wash
up in full color: Like that day in the ER when
they wheeled me away. You followed—your
devotion steady and quiet, obvious. It's un-
reasonable to give each other our everything,

because you've got to be you and I can only
be me. So, you can't have my last cigarette.
But you can have the first cup of coffee. In case
of your moments of doubt, let me make this vow:
there will always be beer and bacon in our fridge.

LIFE GOALS

Accused of misusing color, wasting
ink, wasting paper, I stand fast. I stand
here, at a distance, transcribing my truth
of the matter onto oddly numbered pages:

A faded rose, poetically.
A bony tree, smoldering.
A pair of crippled hands.
A full moon casting a new shadow,
and so on. Violet sky. Wounded smile.

Each image is framed with care by
wide brush-stroked crimson. Each image
is mine, for a lifetime.